# BEFORE
## THE PALM
## COULD BLOOM

# The New Issues Press Poetry Series

| | |
|---|---|
| Editor | Herbert Scott |
| Associate Editor | David Dodd Lee |
| Advisory Editors | Nancy Eimers, Mark Halliday<br>William Olsen, J. Allyn Rosser |
| Assistant to the Editor | Rebecca Beech |
| Assistant Editors | Scott Bade, Allegra Blake, Becky Cooper,<br>Jeff Greer, Gabrielle Halko, Matthew Hollrah,<br>Nancy Hall James, Alexander Long,<br>Tony Spicer, Bonnie Wozniak |
| Editorial Assistants | Kevin Oberlin, Matthew Plavnick<br>Diana Valdez |
| Business Manager | Michele McLaughlin |
| Fiscal Officer | Marilyn Rowe |

The New Issues Press Poetry Series is sponsored by The College
of Arts and Sciences, Western Michigan University, Kalamazoo, Michigan

*An Inland Seas Poetry Book*

mc aca  Inland Seas poetry books are supported by a grant from
The Michigan Council for Arts and Cultural Affairs.

First Edition, 1998.

ISBN:      0-932826-64-4

Library of Congress Cataloging-in-Publication Data:
Wesley, Patricia Jabbeh
Before the Palm Could Bloom/Patricia Jabbeh Wesley
Library of Congress Catalog Card Number (98-066491)

| | |
|---|---|
| Art Direction | Tricia Hennessy |
| Design: | Lisa Ermatinger |
| Cover Photography: | Alfonso Quiroga<br>*Untitled*, photograph, 10" x 10", gelatin silver print |
| Production: | Paul Sizer<br>The Design Center, Department of Art<br>College of Fine Arts<br>Western Michigan University |
| Printing: | Bookcrafters, Chelsea, Michigan |

# BEFORE
## THE PALM
## COULD BLOOM

**POEMS OF AFRICA**

PATRICIA JABBEH WESLEY

New Issues Press

WESTERN MICHIGAN UNIVERSITY

*To the memory of Bai Douju Jabbeh, Toe Jabbeh, my late grandfather,*
*Bai Kpadah (old father) who was not too frail*
*to inspire in me the dream to be a writer.*

*and*

*To my four children—Besie-Nyesuah, Mlen-Too II (MT),*
*Gee, and Ade-Juah Wesley who allow me the time to write*
*while keeping my office as mother.*

# Contents

## III

## Envoi

## Acknowledgments

I am indebted to the following:

The people of Liberia, whose courage compels me
to keep writing.

My father, Moses Chee Jabbeh, who bought me my first
typewriter when I was in elementary school. Your excitement
has been my inspiration.

The Liberian Association of Writers(LAW) in whose midst I grew.

My tenth grade English teacher at the College of West Africa
(CWA), in Monrovia, Dr. Similih H. Cordor, for years
of encouragement.

My husband, Mlen-Too Wesley, my critic, editor, audience
and best friend.

Grateful acknowledgement is made to the editors of the
following publications:

The Liberian Association of Writers (LAW) *Journal*, 1987,
    for "Monrovia Women" and "Heritage."

Michigan College English Association (MCEA) *Journal*, 1996,
    for "In This House."

The author wishes to thank the Irving S. Gilmore Emerging Artist
Grant Program and the Arts Council of Greater Kalamazoo for
their support.

## Africa

The calabash
now shattered

her contents
spilled
like palm wine

across the regions
of the world.

I

## I Am Not *Dekuah*

*Dekuah: come to die*

*Dieh*, I come knocking.
Clansmen, I come calling.
I come crawling at your doors.
There is a matter
from my heart.
Gather your sons from afar
at *Tuwa Kai*.
*Kwee* must come to town today.

Let your sons know my heart.
My heart bleeds blood
thicker than blood.
I am not *Dekuah*;
let me live.

You call me *Dekuah*,
*Mundi, Sejlah, Kahien*,
but I am not.
I've never been born before.
At the coming out of the new moon
I was conceived
to new rice fields, corn on cobs
upon mothers' backs, fresh,
born in the fragrance at harvest.
I am not *Dekuah*.

Why celebrate my coming
with black *lappas* and strange names?
Do you hope by this I will find
my stool in my mother's house?
Where is the Grebo mark, slashed

9

on to your last *Dekuah's* fore-face,
the gash at her earlobes?
My name is *Nehklon*.
Let me live.

Do you reward me,
a new life,
giving me names fit only for death?
Who says I am the yellow-skinned girl
that wiggled in your arms last year?
How could I be the son
who swallowed his breath
before he was washed?
Why trouble me with sharp blades?
Will these poured libations purify the earth?
Will the baobab drink
this wine poured at its roots?
I am not *Dekuah*.

Should I take a stand
in the market place, at the center
of town? Knock old pans together,
blow a horn, a town crier?
Should I pound the drums,
sit upon the king's stool?
I am not *Dekuah*.
Let me live.

Is there none
to pound the drums for a child
forsaken at the birthing house
after the cutting of the navel string?
Old women, their aged wisdom,

refuse the dawn
creeping upon us.
Should I pound my own drums?
*Dieh*, *Bodior,* kinsfolk,
take me to town.
I am not *Dekuah*.

## Tugbakeh: A Song

A ripened breadnut hits the ground
at the outskirts of town.
Tugbakeh boys, half-clothed, run, a game.
Who will be the first to find
its smashed fruit, one of its kind?
Seeds scattered beneath the intermingling
of giant mango, banana and orange trees.

War dancers in raffia skirts
jingling belled ankles, stamping
village dust in the dusky December day.
*Dorklor* is so hard to dance
when veteran dancers are in the lead.
*Gbor-belloh*, too, here he comes,
red rock chalks and charcoal paint
pasted onto his cheeks; his face, a scary mask.
He pulls out his tongue,
stretching it into a mile about himself.
Only the aged can explain
as onlookers run indoors.

The Dodo flaps her wings,
her song for the young that were just hatched.
The white doves will come home for Christmas
to hear her young sing.

Elders, chewing red kola nut,
laugh loudly; proverbs are talking
under the cotton tree. Sipping palm wine
as drums rock the ground
in an earthquake of festivals
older than the earth.
Trumpets follow.

Then come the town's women, renowned.
Years buried under hanging eyelids.
Feet, slapping graciously the ground.
Hips rocking in defiance
of age, arms swinging.
These *Bor-juo-eh* dancers' feet
dance life into this soil.

Kwee will come to town today,
before the Town Crier calls home
the night.
When *Kwee* begins singing,
near the outskirts of town,
*Kwa-jah-lea* will sound.
Women and children will run for doors.
Doors will be latched
when *Kwee* makes his way here.
The old men and the young men
will find laughter again.
Women will be born, will grow breasts
and find men. Will birth babies
for men, then find age when teeth fall out.
Women will lean lightly against their canes
and go gracefully to dark graves
never setting eye upon *Kwee*.

The Dodo flaps her wings,
her song for the young that just learned to fly.
Some day they will fly away
and join the chorus of dodo songs.

Drum pounders sit in that line
at *Tuwah Kai*, under the baobab tree, pounding.

Short drums, tall drums, drums with wide bottoms,
long-legged drums, patient drums. Pounders sweat
as though they are the ones pounded.
Village children run screaming, chanting,
following dancers, overtaken by their dance.

&ast;  &ast;  &ast;

Now Tugbakeh, like a stillborn, stilled.
No arguments for those slapping life
into its wrinkled bottom.
The breadnut still falls, though, and the breadfruit too.
The cocoa and mangoes are full, fruit falling,
smashed, piling under overgrown brushes,
abandoned in the sudden rush of war.

Kola nuts are full now, ripened
by empty suns, half moons, years.
And the coconut trees now touch the skies.
On the ground, dried coconuts
are sprouting everywhere.
Every now and then a mango hits the ground.
Worms and groundhogs have much to eat.
Palm branches still wave, though,
and the wind blows from Tugbakeh's hills.
The forest has taken the streets
from us who used to own the forest.

The Dodo flaps her wings,
her dirge for the young that were not hatched.
An owl on the cotton tree branch
rolls its coconut eyes.

Where did the village folk go?
The elders who used to drag their long *Khaflahs*
on red, dusty, Grebo ground
in the harvest drumming?
Where did the women go?
Their heads that could balance
a pail of water while their arms
swung, or held on to infants falling
out the *lappa's* grip on their backs.
Where are the young girls who held time
in the folding of their palms?
Chalked cheeks, painted for village boys to see.
Eyes with long, bushy lashes.
Careless girls; polished faces.

## The Storm

*To Victims of the Liberian Civil War*

I bent down,
stooping.
Stepped aside.
Crawled
like a crab.
Snailed
into a shell.
I hid, a leech
under a green leaf.
I quit talking
quit breathing
quit laughing.
I waited
for the storm to pass.

## Child Soldier

1.
Child of Liberia, Kahieh,
murdered in Harper
while your dreams bloomed, afresh
at midday.
Just before the palm could bloom;
before the bamboo shoot could spring out.
The brushfire set your branches ablaze.
The palm branch sprang out,
but the fire threatened in the brush—
palm nuts burning in Pleebo
so the planting season
will bring us a great harvest.
The palm branches caught in the brushfire.
Kernels still white, their tender shells, burning.
Gbolobo's tropics lending its young
so warriors will reap
crops they did not plant.

2.
Child of Liberia, Saye,
in Buotuo, you went
with doubting feet
that swayed to the rocking that broke
the dancers' feet.
Running, orphaned early,
where Tapeta takes us to the Gbi forest.
Child soldier, cutting the rope
that ties us to oak branches; branches
to trunks. These oaks
without which history is lost.

3.
Ghapu, Liberia's green palm,
you came from Bassa, trampling the coastline,
carrying adjustable ammunition
in our adjustable age.
I followed your footprints
along Sinoe's beaches, searching to know you.
Child soldier, called to war,
slashing your fathers, cutting off the root
that brings us water from river banks;
this root that calls the Cestos to the Atlantic.
Wlemunga, child warrior,
you for whom history waits
so we can end our anger.
You fell and fell until all lay silent
and bare.
Dying with eyes awake.
History will want to know.
History will want to know.

4.
Child of war, Kortu, my child
who followed where the road led
so crookedly from Nimba to Cape Mount.
From Ganta to Monrovia's rocky hills,
trampling the Mesurado swamps.
Your feet dug deep, printing
stories along Monrovia's hillsides.
Too early beckoned,
you followed too hastily
to grave mounds of dead warriors
in Firestone rubber bush.
Graveyards followed your footprints.

Gravestones, invisible to the passerby.
Our war children,
who follow men who have lost all reason.
Our war
that will not yield to the
cries of newborns, abandoned.


5.
This, my child, my Kahien,
called by our warlords—
our punishment for sins past—
who came demanding our sons
while we still carried them in young wombs.
Our sons, called by our *war heroes,*
blinded by gun dust calling
for more children
though we were quickly made barren by battle.
Calling out for you, Kahien,
a sacrifice to gods who seek
more blood at the hand of more blood.


6.
My child, your nostrils
still full of early dawn mucus,
wetting your pants and bleeding,
wetting Liberia with your bleeding.
The adjustable automatic guns, handed you
at the killing of your father.
Our sons, our history made adjustable
in this adjustable age where
reason loses ground to insanity.
Child soldiers, our children.
Saye, Ghapu, Kahieh, Nimley, Kortu, Wlemunga...

## Finding My Family

"Good friend, please help me.
Did you happen to see
two boys when you lived in Kakata?
One dark, chubby?
The other, light with dark eyes?
Good friend,
did you see them while you lived in Ganta?
One would have been ten
and the other this tall.
My big boy, Nyema, the small one, Doeteh.
Good friend, can you tell me
if they went to Tapeta?
Were they given weapons; did they kill?
Good friend, can you say
if they walked to Bassa?
Did they starve to death?
Good friend, can you say
if there was a mother walking by their side?
Was she healthy? Was she treated well?
Oh, good friend, so this is where
they took them out of line?
Good friend, were they hungry
when they met their end?
Oh, good friend, I will follow
to wrap up their bones.
Thank you, good friend.
But how will I know their bones?

## War Children

*Bury them-oh, we buried them.*
*Bury them-yah! We buried them.*

After years, we now dump those
we used to carry on wheel barrows,
legs and arms dangling, the air
charged with gunfire.
Mothers dragged their young along Duport Road
looking for a decent burial ground.
There is no burial ground anymore.
In their shallow graves the corpses
dance Liberia's cradles empty.

That was then; before the land
turned upon us in anger. Before the earth
refused us burial ground.
Our soil, now soiled, we dig no more.
In digging, we could open up deep sores
in places long closed.
Our people say, *"the hen that scratches too hard*
*digs up its mother's bones."*

## Warrior

I am Tagbe-Toe,
come home from war.
But the kola nut tree
dropped its flowers
during the storms.
There are no greetings,
and I'm left at the door post
by my own clansmen.

The women are gathered
at the backyard with
water-filled kola nut bowls.
But there are no kola nuts
for this spicy pepper
in earthen jars.
And here I sit alone
at the door post,
smelling its pungent odor.

Gbolobo has given in
to government troops;
our warriors' heads
crushed with guns.
Their brains thrown into the Gbi forest
to fertilize the land
so Tubman may some day
sell our timber.

There is no war song;
no drums to sound
a warrior's return.
But will the kola nut
not greet me
in my own town?

If I were *Yarkpawollo*
I would climb a palm tree,
a gun at my shoulder,
pointed at the innocent, too.
But mine is just a quiet homecoming
as I await my greetings
at the doorpost.

# Have You Been Felled?

*Upon hearing of the capture and killing of their leader*

So, here you are.
Cobra. Lion.
You who never knew your own mortality.
Have you been felled?

Aye-yah, how can we stop
this wailing, now,
how can we stop the weeping?
We gave our hearts to you,
but did you dash them in Liberia's swamps?
Our sons came running to greet you
in the harvest dance,
but did you give our sons back to us
scattered along shelled roadways?

"Lock the doors;
shield the women
away."
We shut the doors,
but your latch
let our children
and our women out,
sent them floating
like cork wood
in the Cavalla, the Loffa,
Sinoe, Mesurado, St. Paul.

How can we stop the weeping?
May I have a drink?

Are you like me, a wanderer?
Is your night thundery
dark, and fierce, no one
to greet you
as you seek a stool
on which to sit
with your kinsmen?

We tell the stories now,
stories you said we
would not live to tell.
We tell them, you see,
just as you wished them told,
with gunfire and decomposed corpses,
people silenced,
in your redemption.
Liberians, forever
in need of redemption.

Aye-yah!
May I have a drink?

Why did you bring us tears, too,
with the poverty? We love the poverty
better than the tears, you know.

Have you been felled?
Left for dogs,
for true-true-true,
left for dogs?
The flies are full now.
The dogs died in time,
having eaten away your enemies
and your brothers, too.

How can we end this wailing?

May I borrow your child
so she may fetch me a pail of water
from the stream?
May I borrow your daughters,
your wife, your mother,
that they may wail over my bones?
Your sons
that they may bury my bones?

My brother lay dying.
The flies singing
a love song to his body.
Oh, the faithfulness of flies!

Have you been felled?

I am so thirsty.
Did they give me kola nuts yet?
Let the pepper be burning hot, spiced
with my mother's mother's spice.
Why isn't the kola nut bitter?
Is my mouth turning bitter too?
I like the thirst instead.

Look behind our house.
Did you see the kola nut hole?
Did they dump my brothers
in the kola nut hole?
How can we end this wailing?
May I have a drink?

## Oh Rivers : Nov. 7,1995

*To the memory of Nyenbe Wesley, my brother-in-law*
*and Nyanken Hne Boah, my cousin*

You gulped down my brothers,
my sisters
my children
in your deep throats;
down your intestinal tubes
that lead to the Atlantic.
Oh Cavalla
Oh Sinoe!
Oh Loffa
Oh St. John!
Oh St. Paul
Oh Mesurado!
What is it
we have done to you?
Your secrets
will someday be known
when you burst forth
with all the bones
of those swallowed up
in your deep bellies.
Oh Cestos, Oh Dugbe,
Oh Mano.

## What Dirge

So what shall I use to wipe my brow?
To bring back a life
snatched away in its prime?
What shall I say, and what shall I lay hands
so helpless upon to wipe the sorrow
from my brow?

What shall I wear to mourn a life
whose end has dealt us this blow?
Shall I wear black, so when our townswomen,
hearing the drums, come wailing, wailing,
they shall see the sorrow
of my heart on my dark *lappa*?

Shall I tie a string around my forehead?
Shall I lie prostrate on *The Mat*?
Shall I cry tears for those you've left us to feed
when we ourselves cannot feed ourselves
in a land where the hungry, forever hungry,
keep the faith?

What dirge shall I sing?
Shall I recount the battles fought at *Nganlun*?
Shall I sing of blood shed at the cracking of a gun
when I myself am so afraid of the gun?
What shall I say when the women,
hearing my song, come wailing
and knocking at my door?

II

## Strange Lovers

So it is the moon that sends the Mesurado
running to visit the Atlantic
with its millions of troops?

Why can't these troops of river fish say
to such constant interruption
of a good day's work:

*"What do you want with us, oh river,
oh Atlantic?"*

But you go running as soon as the
moon relays its message
in the language of rivers.

You never ask if it is fine with me,
your neighbor.
Running off,
as though you were betrothed to her.

You never ask if I would love to keep
company with your fish.
Taking off in flight any time of day.

I come walking to see you.
I come with kola nuts, though it is your place
to greet me so. But there you are, gone again
to your lover, the Atlantic.

One of these days when you return
from rendezvous too subtle for human minds,
I'll be gone,

I say, gone to unknown lands
where rivers know their places
in deep beds, where loneliness kills their young
at conception.

I'll be gone, like the wife wearied of waiting
for an unfaithful husband leaves before
the break of dawn.

Like a frog that cried and cried for the rain,
and before the rains, withers beside the dried
banks of the stream.
I'll be gone, Mesurado, do you hear me?

# Heritage

My home is *Nganlun*;
sparkling *Nganlun*, emptying
its wealth of fisheries into *Sehn*, singing,
flowing between rocks and hills.
*Nganlun*, that caused the wanderer to stay,
the traveler to make home here in Tugbakeh.
Our thirst quencher, life giver, rushing
as if beckoned by a sacred call.
*Nganlun* runs in my blood,
between joints, and in my tissues,
flowing freely in my heart,
pumping blood to my brain and vessels.

Tugbakeh, that's home!
Where our family rope entangles us
in a spider's web, where we love and fight,
bending the *Toebo* family tree during
heavy family storms.
My father's father, and his father's father's father,
Bai Toe, called you home, this Tugbakeh
of aged trees in the red earth
looming over the narrow road
that leads to Harper.

My name is Jabbeh. *Jabbeh Cho*,
in a forest, hunting, the tornado mistook him
for a bunch of palmnuts, saved him
amidst the howling in the trees.
In me, he turned up dark, me, ebony,
after an endless line of *Toebos*
had passed on.
This long string of *Toebos*, on various rocky routes.
At a dead-end in us women.
But in our brothers, the branching roots.

## Big Ma

Big Ma, *Khadi*, *Nyene-Wheh*.
Our cook spoon and *fufu* stick, our dipper, too.
Blinded by the smoky kitchen.
Dishing out with a nod of her head
the boiling pot of palmnut soup
over steaming cassava.
A black pot burns her right hand.
She reaches for a dish rag; she wipes the pain
from her watering eyes.

*Khadi-Wheh*, the holder of hot pots.
Her children come home from school
and Ma is steaming up the house
with spiced peppers, sweet blossoms
in a pot of Plato sauce.
Blessed, her movement, graceful, heavy; her mind
far away with our uniforms for Flag Day,
boots for the rain, our school books.
There's an aroma of bay leaves and basil, beaten
in peppers, in the house.
Her heart is heavy, but the rice is fluffy.

She wraps a string around
her *lappa* and her stomach, to hold her hunger
that we children may nibble
a piece of cassava, a bite of coco yam.
Ma, *Khadi Nyene*, her own emptiness
she refills with a large cup of water.
When we cry, she rubs us
against her belly, singing, "*Take Time In Life*."

Watch woman for mosquitoes,
peering at the window, talking to the thunder

though the storm is far from home,
even in September.
The rains hit, she walks from room to room
looking for the leak. Thunder rumbles;
lightning, she jerks.
In the middle of the night, by the window
overlooking the sea, she watches
the night slowly fall asleep.
A rooster crows, another follows,
a twilight in the distance
falling upon the ocean.
Another day, we will call her blessed.

# Knowing

You who know the taste of *kitile*
or bitter balls and bamboo shoots

though you have tasted sugar cane
harvested from the hills

know that sugar cane
from the hills has its taste

but the swamps will give us another cane;
*kitile* and bitter balls can be just as sweet.

You who know how the rain sounds
when it hits a thatched roof

know that though a roof is made of zinc
sometimes we love the thatch

more than we love the zinc.

## To: *Bai* Jabbeh

On a bamboo, wobbling chair, he sat.
*Khaflah*, bundled up at belly button,
dragged upon dusty, village floor.
A patient chair bearing this wisdom;
after years had taken their share,
we had this much of him.

His tales stood upon a hill, tall,
bringing us history in a scoop.
Hitler's planes flew all about us,
but the allies shot them down.
War history of Grebo revolts triumphant.
We sat staring as wars were fought all about us
in the middle of Borbor Tugba's house.

I saw years drain rivers around
*Bai*'s wrinkled eyelids, the allies' planes bombing
and shelling Japan and Germany.
Hitler, defeated in one strike.
By now *Bai* was up, standing
on wobbling legs, young again
as Hitler lay dead,
and we children cheered.

I loved those other tales
when elephants, leopards and lions leapt
out of Tugbakeh's jungles.
I sat close to his wobbling chair;
*Bai* waved away flies
and baptized us with saliva of wisdom,
spinning up another leg of a tale.

# In Memory of Cousin Hazel: A Dirge

*December 1988*

Come and see me
who has buried herself.
Death has been cruel to me
from my youth.
And now that I am gray
I have dug into this red earth
and laid my navel string
into a hole so deep.

When the cock crows
I feel myself stirring
under the red earth.
My only girl is laid to rest,
and here I stand, wailing
over the hole
that has swallowed
my heart away.

My girl has gone
and done
what a woman doesn't do.
Has let her breath slip
while she brought forth life.
Our people say,
*"one doesn't die in childbirth."*
So now my child
will never come to town again
to roll my *Mat* away.

40

## African Death

So pleased now, that smile, curved
tightly around his kola polished teeth.
He had always wanted to wear a suit,
a dark suit, tie and all.
Had always dreamt of being cuffed
and primed and collared in white;
had dreamt his feet
that had so gracefully eaten the red
village soil would someday be sheltered
in these shoes now sheltering his toes.
How glad he hadn't died in the bombing
like everybody else.

He, who would have never worn a suit,
and a dark suit at that!
He, who would have never had his enemies
praise him so. Had never before seen
such fussing as they are doing now for his death.
Fussing about what he'd wear on his way to Heaven.
Why hadn't he known they loved him better
in a wooden box?

Look at him now, how dignified,
how respectable, their city way.
Maybe they'll send along his old pants
in case this clothing was borrowed
for the eyes of the dead living.
Maybe they want him not greeting God
in shabby pants.
Oh, why had he taken so long to see
they loved him dead?

Now they are cooking
and singing those heroic dirges of old.
Slapping their chests, falling all over the floor.
His daughters have not had a meal in days.
Look at his sons, all lined up,
standing up to death, these African sons,
oh, stop that!

They are now fussing about the usual
African things that crop up like rice at funerals.
Look at them, standing there, grieving,
the African way, so full of glamour.
Oh, death, you are so honorable
and so gracious.
How glad he wasn't left along
the way for dogs that chewed
so many honorable bones.
How blessed to have had these daughters,
on *The Mat* now, so proud of a dead father.
Life should have given him a hint, a knock on
the shoulder bone, a bang on the head.
If he had seen all the trophies death brings
he would have died in even better times.

Then will come the drums, the wake-keeping,
coffee brewing, even though he'd
never known the taste of coffee.
Then will come all the biscuits on silver trays
passed around while the church choir hums
those traditional songs of old.
And those *Conger* wake-keeping songs
will be sung with dragging tones.

And then will come the long obituaries, his
sons proud of all he'd done, and not done,
and his death. Then the marching, the wailing
to the grave. All the sisters, those faithful ones,
will borrow tears from other deaths.
Then, at the grave, the sermon for a man
who'd never known the face of God.
And the daughters, arm in arm, around
his lovely new home, wailing and threatening
to follow, oh, stop that!
Who ever told him death was painful?

He'd probably break up in a loud laugh.
Death, you are so humorous, so very humorous.
Then, after the wailing, the hollering,
the fussing, the sons and daughters
will return to their lives, their new lives
in the cities, their cities that have burnt
down the villages and his life.
Gracefully, they will return,
leaving him under the care of death,
in a dark suit, and a smile sheltering
his brown teeth.

## Take Me Way Back

Take me way, way back, I say, years.
Pick me up, strap me onto your wide back.
I want to roll back tears and years.
When we girls wore pony tails.
They say we were green girls, but hip.
We girls, not knowing the taste of a boy's lips
on our lips, ah-hah!

"*Ah- Sama-lay- kou-lay, Ah-Sama-lay-kou-lay*,"
we screamed and danced at football games.
Our boys, chasing the running ball,
we girls, chasing them.
Yes, and let the games end, my, my.
We crowded over sweating boys
like driver ants over rotten palmnuts
on the ground, beneath a palm tree.

Man, take me back, my people!
And let Flag Day come!
You think there was time to ask why it rained
so hard on Flag Day?
The bands mingled with drums, the sound
of raindrops and feet tapping as we

marched down Broad Street, up Ashmun Street,
the rocky hill of Mamba Point.

44

We girls in uniforms of blue skirts, green
skirts, white or yellow blouses, soiled.
Boys, in peaceful blue pants
clinging to long thighs in the August rain.

Then comes college, oh, my Lord, take me back!
We girls, in college? Free as the air to roam wild,

Monrovia's hills like mushrooms.
We quickly found more boys: short boys, tall boys,
light-skinned boys, midnight-skinned, brought them home.

Thin boys with large eyes, their beards
thick like raffia. Blended in books with boys;
married real fast as Mama wished.
And other girls, you see, they stood there, watching.
Stole other girls' men, oh my!
But some of us girls, Miss booky brains,
birthed babies like church rats.

## Monrovia Women

Monrovia women . . .
Here they come!
You see their colorful faces
before you know their hearts.
Shining, red lips, red cheeks,
painted eyelids and lashes.
Perhaps they would like
to paint their pupils, too!
Their eyebrows take to various routes
to suit their longing hearts.

*Aye,* Monrovia women . . .
Look at their necks!
You could build a mansion
from jewelry a single woman wears.
Sometimes, like Indians,
their noses wear gold rings,
while their ears themselves
wear several others too.

You have yet to see their hands . . .
Long nails painted
to match the various hues
their eyes and cheeks wear.
Fingers held apart
by heavy gold rings.
Oh, you should see them
walking down the road.

Monrovia women . . .
In evening gowns and dresses,
*lappa* suits and costly coats,
on their way to work.

You should see them at work!
They nurse and paint their nails all day,
and guide their skirts from hooking
on to a rustic nail.

Monrovia women . . .
Strolling in the humid sun
in high, expensive shoes.
If you would stop
to ask their toes
how much fun it really is,
walking in such heels,
I'm sure you'd say *aye-yah*,
for our poor Monrovia women.

## Nyanken Hne

My husband, Nyanken Hne,
like *galo*, waving up Dolokeh's hills.
The storms cannot touch him;
they fear him like a wife fears a jealous man.
The young girls with their shining eyes,
whose lashes wave, stand off the road
when Nyanken Hne passes.
Their pails of water fall off their heads
to see Nyanken Hne pass by.

My husband, Nyanken Hne,
who came amidst polished smiles, long,
dark, chalked faces, bowing when he passes.
Nyanken came, dancing my way,
in a war dance, shining like ebony.
How I love to look at him dancing
to giant drums beating in the dusky wind.
How Nyanken passed them all by
while they called him with swinging
oiled, brown arms, dancing.
But Nyanken chose only me.

Nyanken has said I am the only one.
He has broken taboos, has shattered
their good dreams.
All these years, Nyanken has said, no,
I am the only one.
When I rise, Nyanken is there,
like the mighty, rising *Sebo*.
Unlike our townsmen whose eyes
never quit hunting, Nyanken has only me.
When I sit, he looks down into my eyes,
and they all stand and stare.

## They Say

Liberian women say
Men are like the stick
of a cassava plant
with many eyes. Yet
cannot see

when worthy women
pass them
along the way.
They say
Liberian men
are a river,
meandering,
sometimes
flooding the land.
Like the Mesurado,
they say,
in every backyard.
You must not trust
Liberian men.

What do you say
to such and such?
*"I saw your man drive by;*
*another woman in the front.*
*I saw your husband*
*smiling in her face.*
*And worst of all,*
*she rolled her eyes.*
*I saw her*
*last jawbone teeth,*
*smiling at your man."*
What would you make
of this, my friend?

*Aye-yah, my dear,*
*Men are like*
*cassava sticks,*
Liberian women say.

## I'm Still Thinking . . .

Today I prayed for you to die
in the July downpour, the rain
beating down aluminum zinc roofs,
into gutters, turning red
upon muddy hillsides. You, drowned
in the St. Paul River. Rain water
from Monrovia's hills will meet you
at the arteries of St. Paul.
Waves washing you up and down
like children playing see-saw.

Divers won't find you, but
the gigantic sea crabs will. They'll snip
your toes, one by one, then your fingers—
your Ma, sitting on *The Mat*, waiting, hoping.
And those divers, arriving each day, heads bowed,
they'll say, "We didn't find his body."

Oh, no, God, don't let him die that way.

Today I prayed you'll just drop and die.
They'll lay you up like a real corpse.
You've always been a corpse. You, Dave,
stretched out like an ironed gown
in a wooden box painted black with tar.
Face wrinkled from cheating on us girls.
Flies everywhere, singing, and we girls standing
at a distance in high-heeled shoes,
silky, pink blouses, sweet perfumed hair, and
laughing loudly.

Oh, no, God, don't let him die that way.

You kept me standing, Dave, waiting.
Lace trimmings running down
my wedding gown, me waiting. Eternally.
I still wait at weddings, Dave, for you.

Lord, let him live, waiting on death.

You will rot, waiting on women. Your wife
will dish you up on a plastic platter to eat,
your yelling wife, a beast, cooking you half
cooked meals.
Birthing you half-hearted babies, beating you up
with a leg from your dining table.

You'll meet me and my husband, a real man,
down Randall Street. You, standing there,
wrinkled with age.
Oh no, God, don't let him live that way.

I pray, today, wait a minute God, I'm still thinking.

## Outside Child

Her husband comes home, bringing in
this roll of blanket, arms around it, a ball.
Red fingers poking out, reaching.
*What is that?* She says. This man,
immobile; feet upon marble floor, and
the sunlight here, finding its way through

windows; rays dancing, curtains swaying
to the Atlantic breeze that visits Sinkor
at sunset. She takes this bundle,
peeps into its pink face; cheeks, puffy and red,
a pyramid of a head,
brown eyes, brown lashes, no hair, a human?

She unwraps it like a silly child
opening a long desired birthday gift, fearful
of what it contains.
This wiggling thing, a child, a boy child, screaming?
*Is he motherless?* She holds him to her breast.
This thing that will rob her of heart and mind.

Her husband stands like a tree
after lightning has struck. Lips glued
on to teeth, tears streaming down wrinkled
cheeks, arms wide, begging.
But for what?
She stands there, hugging this child,
talking to this stranger in a blanket.

*My child*, he tells her; this man,
bringing her a child like this from the outside?
After long nights, loud bars, gin,
whisky, beer cans and women?

Her oven heart, her furnace.
This man comes bestowing a child upon her?
*Is this what I win?* She asks.
Having cooked him spicy *torgborgee*,
*kpassajama*, okra, stewed with scrimps,
pig's feet, smoked salmon,
bush hog-meat, bony fish, wild chicken legs?
Poured upon fluffy rice, *fufu*,
cassava steamed to taste?
For fixing him up during the flu or
malaria evenings? Giving him babies?
Putting up with his family, uncountable

in numbers and ways?
Her husband brings in this alien thing?
*Where is his mother?* She screams.
But he stands there, watching curtains
around them dance.
*Answer me, where is she?*

## This Rooster Will Come Home to Roost

This rooster will come home to roost.
Scratching and scattering, feet roasted by travel.
Scratch your way home, rooster, red like the evening
setting behind early night. Did you miss your way home?
You must call in the morning, now, loud rooster.

This time, you must rush, the sun is setting, and
those hawks that saw you flee, again will gaze at you.
They will weep hot drops of motor oil tears
for desecrating your life. You, again, must flap
your wings, calling home our dawn.

Flapping your giant wings before the village square
you will crow others homeward.
We need you so dawn will quickly come.
Orange red, black wings, flapping; you, dancing
the rooster dance to barren hens
that were widowed at birth.

## One of These Days

One of these days
there will be rejoicing
all over the place.
There will be so much shouting,
so much wailing,
so much dancing.
There's going to be
such dancing
as we've never before seen
in Monrovia.
There's going to be a day
like that, I say,
and there's no one
who will be able to stop us.

I'm going to train
my feet
for that day.
It's going to be something
in Monrovia's streets,
all potted up with
bullet holes.
Our feet tapping will make
all those holes
vanish just like that,
before we know it.
I can't wait to see the faces
of those who have defied
death all these years.
Man,
I just can't wait.
All those who died
eating

those hot, burning bullets
and all our families
gone, will want us
dancing
and singing again.
Man, I just can't wait.
Where will all those soldiers be
when our drums
break through the air?
You mean
all those villages
laid bare by bullets?
Those cities, flattened
by their rockets?
Man,
It's going to be something!

All of us refugees
will come home again;
and we will cook
on *26th day* again.
palm butter and rice,
potato greens in one pot,
dried fish, spiced,
the other,
with cassava leaf in red oil.
Old time *kpassajama*! My!
We will steam jollof rice,
*fufu*, paddled with fufu sticks,
*dumb-boy*, pounded hard
in flat mortals again.
The soup, oh man!
We will eat like the good old days.

I bet
the old people
will put *The Mat* down.
The elders
will shout, *"Ba-te-oh,"*
*"Ba."*
about the pot
that was not broken.
Some old women will wail,
or sing a dirge
for those fallen
in this war.

Some orphans
will go out, searching
for those lost loved ones,
hoping they are alive.
Some of us may weep.
Sometimes,
tears can heal.
But Man,
after all the wailing
there's got to be some laughter
with the tears.

Com' on,
get ready for the dancing
and hollering
in the streets of Monrovia.
Man, Monrovia, we're coming.
We will dance,
and dance down Waterside
with all its rocky hills and traffic.

Its crowded market stalls,
heavy Big Mamas, *grona* boys and thieves.
All its corrugated zinc shacks,
Waterside life.
I'm waiting until
they put this wild fire out.
Sometimes, I just can't wait
to put my feet to the test.
Who can say the kind of dancing
when this flame
is out, oh, Man!

## Minority

At home,
I am a Jabbeh, *Jabbeh Cho*,
married to *Suo Paton*, now a Wesley.
A *Toebo*, from *Gbaplepoe Paton*,
*Chee Dawanyeno*, *Jlajeh*. *Bodior* line.
A *Tuo*, from *Tugbakeh*, of *Whyne* lineage,
where the Jabbehs have their place
in the history of the Grebo people.
I am Grebo,
the Grebos, coming down
the Grebo Forest, seeking the coastline.
The Grebos of the *Gbolobo War*,
the *Grebo Wars*
against Americo-Liberian dominion.

At home,
I am not only Grebo.
A Marylander of Marylanders.
I have never before
stumbled my way
into history.
I come from where
the Atlantic refuses to sleep.
Where the forest never turns yellow.
Where the waters run wild, cold.
Where the brooks sing a melody
to the sea.
Where the Cavalla rushes to greet
the ocean with kola nuts
and spiced pepper.
Maryland, where Cape Palmas
borrows land to the sea,
stretching its arm
to greet the sea.

I am Kwa,
A Kwa of Kwas,
where the Krus, the Grebos,
the Krahns, the Sapos,
the Bassas and the Belles
come from a common shoot.
We are a people
of all peoples.
Our lines run deep,
deeper than the soil
that meets the waters across West Africa.
In Africa, I am Liberian.
When I speak, I give myself away,
a Liberian.

I am African,
West African,
of Songhai, Mali and Ghana,
a huge history, smeared with blood,
the blood of slavery.
We are Cain of Africa.
The sons of Jacob.
Having sold our kin to Egypt,
we've come to meet them.
Yes, they are our kin.
They look like us.
They even dance like us,
and laugh like us
and cry like us.
So America puts us together
in America's jar, a tight jar.
Minority.
Ah, what a word!

## My Wife Brings Home Another Husband

Lawns will grow green after this snow.
The wood pile beside our home will lie in wait.
But a new man walks in,
tall, lingering like an aged palm tree in
September's storms.
Eyes pale blue, a knife-pointed nose.
Silky, red hair flying about a thin face.
He smiles, and my mind chases butterflies.
*Did my wife bring home*
*another husband to husband her and me?*

"Oh father, did you say, slap her?
A woman like Musu in America?
Do you want to see your son again before
the grave comes graciously calling you?"

"Meet Jim," my wife tells me, clinging to this,
her Jim. He rubs her shoulders that I may see
with my two eyes. Blood rushes to her cheeks
like clouds, and I stare at her,
here between us husbands.
The blood of my heart pours down my legs.
We are about to drown in my blood, and
yet I stand

here, looking. My life, now a mere piece of paper,
shredded. My marriage
returned to me as if an old friend had
simply refused a gift from my hand.
My life spread out on *The Mat*,
and here I stand
in this warm room, and the snow creeping in.
"Musu", I hear myself murmur, but the husband

stands there, hugging the wife, our wife.
In our home, Father, firewood
warms the soul; this, our neighborhood
where smoking chimneys rise to the skies.
My wife here in this deep snow
no longer needs her father's blessings
to wed another husband?
This woman, bringing home this man
while I still lie at her breast?

My wife, her dark eyes that held me captive.
This Musu, who dabbles away shame with
long, dark lashes; her yellow face, immaculate.
Long fingers carved to perfect hands;
nails, now against the firelight glow.
At the end of three sons, Musu stands there,
and I can almost wrap my two palms about
her silky thinness.
Her skirt, too short for homemade girls.
Yellow daffodils, like butterflies
down its front.
This Musu, so revered at home
marrying another man just like that?

I rush for my coat, Father, I find solace in leather
jackets these days.

Should I have pushed the gentleman out?
This gentleman whose head touches our ceiling?
Hair all over his face, punch him?
*Oh, my coat, where are you?*
The snow stares at me through the window glass.
My life, returned to me through a mere window.
The pine tree at the front, holding so graciously

to snow flakes as if to hurl them at me when I step out.
Then I gather myself from all
the corners of this house to the front door.
As I step through, the door creaks,
ajar.

## Surrender

So often, I want to make you;
roll you, reshape you, a ball of clay
after my say.
I want to squeeze you,
my play dough, an image,
into my image.
I want to melt you, shape you, like gold;
polish you, mold you into a charm
to be sold.

My little woodwork, carve you,
make you my *Kissi* ritual mask.
I want to hang you
so often, around these, my walls,
make you my little talisman,
swing you, my little magic wand.

My pungent, leafy *voodoo*,
my *sumu*, my boiling pot of *juju*.
My little protective pin
about my fabric life, about my pieces.
I want to ride you, my cruising Pajaro.
Suddenly, there
you are, always God.

Now, it is your turn. Here, roll me,
reshape me, pat me, mold me,
heating the clay of my flesh,
after your flesh.

Grip hold of my mascara cheeks, my charms
of gold bracelets, binding my life.
Melt all my magic wands,
my bulging, voodoo eyes.
Take hold of my big, bleeding heart,
my boiling pot of *juju*, my beads
of charms, my me.
And if I'm not yet surrendered,
my God, vanquish me.

## When I Get to Heaven

When I get to heaven
I'm going to shout hallelujah all over the place.
Dancing the *Dorklor*, the *Wahyee*,
the Ballet, the Rock and Roll.
I'll dance the Brake, the Rap, Hip Hop.
All the dances only sinners have danced.
I'll sing Opera, the African way,
dance the Ballet the African way.

When I get to heaven
I'll pray so loud, shaking hands the White way,
the Black way; greeting with kola nuts
as the Grebos do.
I'll lie prostrate, to greet
the Yoruba way. Snap fingers to greet
as Liberians do.
There will be no boundaries, no laws, no rules.

When I get to heaven
I'll sing the blues and dance the *Sumu*.
I'll paint my face with white chalk and red rock,
sit with missionaries so all can see.
I'll pound my drums, shaking my *Sahsah*.
Blowing my trumpet the African way.
Dancing to Jesus the African way.

## I Smell Home

Palm butter leaves, pungent, burning these, my nostrils.
Pepper, hot and spicy, ground up like pudding
or pounded *fufu*, *dumb-boy*, ready to be consumed.

I feel the boiling pot rocking to the heat beneath.
A Grebo woman is cooking.
Somewhere, a Grebo woman is cooking.

Palm butter often gives itself away, even in strange lands.
To speak of dried antelope, kiss meat, river shells and crab
mingling in with fresh palm nut soup.
I smell home in this far away country.

## In This House

In this house
potatoes grow up
with age
and reason;
then grow legs
and arms,
walk out
and leave
our premises.

No one here
eats potatoes.
Even onions
spread themselves thin
like palm fronds,
eventually
grow weary
with age,
following after
the footsteps of potatoes.

We eat rice,
cassavas, and
sweet potatoes
that grow at home.
We steam eddoes
and yams,
pound *fufu*
and let Irish potatoes
move out
into the snow.

## To Michigan

Palm oil redness coming down
across the darkening of Michigan's skies
where day and darkness speak in whispers.
Michigan and Huron meet.

The skies are turning,
peaches piled in a bowl.

Huge drops of palm oil spill
as Huron runs in half leaps,
falling and rising,
wanting to know.

Palm oil skies falling upon pine trees.
Cedar, standing their ground in Cedarville.
After all, this is Cedarville.
These trees have learnt the skill
it takes to stand up to old winter.

Suddenly, there they are, Michigan and Huron
meeting,
waves flying everywhere
as geese begin this loud squawking,
flapping wings and dust.

The lakes are now taking on the color of the skies;
waves falling, touching the twilit skies,
a taste of African palm oil just spilled.

The vastness of the lakes
and the darkening skies
of Michigan, red with palm oil.

# Homecoming

1.
I don't want to be a stranger
when I come home.
Yes, I'm a wanderer,
a woman.
But I don't want to be a stranger
in my hometown.
I will not stand outdoors
waiting in the dark
at the doorpost
of my father's house.
I want the fire place lit.
I want the wood sparkling
with fire balls
when I come home.

2.
I want my kola nuts
handed to me
on earthen platters;
the pepper in earthen jars
spiced, like we know it,
when I come home.
Let them fetch me water
in white pails
from *Nganlun.*
Oh, the coolness of *Nganlun,*
sweet *Nganlun,*
that penetrates the heart.
*Nganlun,*
that never dries up
in the scorching heat of March.

3.
I don't want to stay
the wanderer.
I want my brothers
to take me in.
Let them meet me
at the gateway
of  Toe Whyne's compound.
Let them bow
where libation
would have been poured.
Let them raise hands
to God
for sparing some of us.
When I come home,
I want to be treated
to welcoming songs of praise.
Do not forget my names.
I want my praise names
recited to incessant drumming.
List my names
in their proper order
like our Mothers sang them
when we pestled rice
in wobbling mortars.
Remember our ancestors
for their deeds,
and let their names
grace those songs of praise
in my homecoming.

4.
If they kill all our brothers
who will meet me
when I come home
after this wandering?
Who will keep the wood burning
in our fathers' house?
You see, I am a woman,
the wanderer
made even more so
by war.
When I come home
to my people
I want to see my brothers,
all the sons of *Taabah*,
the greatest of our wanderers,
our mother.
I want her stock
lined up to meet
the new wanderer.
Our fathers gave us brothers
to keep the hut warm,
to keep the family smoke
rising above our roofs
so we can come home.
I am only a woman;
let my brothers live.
Let me come home
again.

Envoi

## The Visiting Artist

Her eyes had not lost their light
in the dark of the refugee camp in Ghana.
Here, the sofa is soft, the lamplight, dim.
But the grant had been specific:
". . . to rehabilitate you."
So here she is, and her patrons, smiling.
They ask her for a song,
the songs she had sung during *Total Involvement
For Higher Heights days*. So she sang.

"This old man had a peculiar mouth;
he was not old, but the inside
of his cheeks touched as if he was old.
His mouth now a smashed papaya;
they made him set his home ablaze,
then shot his family, one by one,
twelve of them, while he watched.
They sent him away.

This little boy you see was there. He saw the power
that banged out the old man's teeth,
that raped his mother; that shot his father, his father
with muscular arms; his father,
that wall of a man, shot without a word.

He asked for the gun,
that gun that held such strength;
now a new god, that gun.
He walked into the crowd
that had drunk from an angry waterfall.
His mother will know him no more.

That old man as toothless as an infant;
that family, shot; that boy, lost among the crowd,
the angry crowd, now thin from war.
My father, my husband, my son, my family,
and here I sing of them over a cup of coffee."

The song is done.
the thin, singing musician stands;
her patrons scramble, seeking
to be rescued by napkins.
They long for a dark night
familiar only to her.
Her host runs, fumbles in the closet for more napkins.
The lamp glows on shadows
against the wall.
A song, emerging from the shadows,
arises, singing of the rest of them;
those whose songs
will never be sung, those whose wives
followed their footsteps
the day the guns seized the towns.

The guest, standing,
her patrons, reluctant to say goodbye.
She walks out to the car waiting at the front yard
where the smell of roses and marigolds mingles
in the spring evening, in the dark.
The song goes on in the lamplight
as napkins console her patrons.

# Glossary

### BODIOR
The High Priest or spiritual head of a Grebo town. He is head of the Tuwah Kai, or holy house, where the shrine and religious relics are kept.

### BORH-JUO-EH
A dance among the Grebo people of Liberia, usually performed by women during the dance of Kahn or Wlee.

### CONGER
A word used to describe an Americo-Liberian or descendent of American freed slaves.

### DEKUAH
A name among the Grebo people usually given to a child who may not live, especially after several infant deaths in the family. The name means "Come to die".

### DIEH
The elders who are the authority, known as the owners of the land.

### DORKLOR
Is a dance associated with the Wlee or Kahn (depending on which area of the Grebo tradition one is speaking of). Otherwise known as the War Dance, this dance is performed by men and women to celebrate victory after war, commemorate death, war, and many other significant occasions such as the honoring of great personalities. There are many dances around Africa, especially West Africa, which are similar to the Dorklor.

## GBOLOBO

Is a town in Maryland County, west of Harper, its capital city. This town is noted for the Gbolobo war with the Liberian government in the 1920s.

## GBOR-BELLOW

The professionally trained magician (artist) and seer who is the officially designated performer, working varying supernatural signs during festivities. He may perform strange wonders under the watchful eyes of hundreds of villagers.

## GREBO (Glebo)

Is an ethnic people of Liberia whose main homeland is Maryland County, in South Eastern Liberia. The Grebos who migrated into this region hundreds of years ago also inhabit parts of Grand Kru County and lower Grand Gedeh County as well as parts of the Ivory Coast along the Cavalla River. The Grebo Language is of the Kwa family of languages.

## KAHN OR WLEE

(War Dance) is the most significant ritual dance among the Grebo ethnic peoples. It is known as the War Dance because hundreds of years ago this was the dance performed before warriors went to battle and after. In modern times, this dance is performed to commemorate a significant birth, death, harvest, marriage, etc. Nowadays, the War Dance is performed even in cities.

## KLAHN—KLAHN-TEH

Is the sound of the wailing, talking drum, the largest and tallest drum in a Grebo town or village. At the pounding, people hundreds of miles away may hear and follow the sound in order to find out why the drum is sounding. The meaning of the sound is "Very important news."

KWEE
The name of the sacred spiritual leader of male society among the Grebo and related ethnic peoples of Liberia. Also the name of the society itself of which Kwee is the leader. He performs such functions as that of law enforcer and spiritual intermediary. He is invisible to women, and it is an abomination, and punishable by death, for a woman or an uninitiated male to see Kwee. According to Grebo mythology, Kwee lives in the spirit world and visits town only to enforce the law or to perform certain rituals. Women have heard his singing, his speeches, but have never seen him.

LAPPA
The wrap-around, or skirt, that is worn by most African women, in Liberia is called Lappa.

THE LIBERIAN CIVIL WAR
The Liberian civil war, which began on December 24, 1989, officially ended in August 1996 with the implementation of the Abuja Peace Accord. The human costs of the war were immense: 200,000 war related deaths, 1.2 million persons displaced internally, and approximately 750,000 refugees in neighboring countries. This from a pre-war population of 2.5 million. The war received only brief and sporadic international notice although it included such atrocities as the massacre of more than 600 people inside Monrovia's downtown Lutheran Church in 1990. As is true in many such wars, ethnic and territorial factors weighed heavily in the advent and continuation of hostilities. This civil war, according to Howard W. French in The New York Times, February 4, 1998, became "a prototype for other African conflicts in the 1990's. Liberia was also a pioneer in the use of children as soldiers." Fifty thousand children were among the war's dead. "But even beyond factors like these, the signal distinction of the Liberian war, and its most disturbing

legacy for this continent, was the notion that combat may, or even should, be waged against unarmed civilians." Mr. French continues with the observation that "in Liberia, where the instigator of the war and leader of its largest faction won a presidential election last year, there has been virtually no movement for an accounting of past atrocities."

THE MAT
Symbolic and also physical, a tradition common among the Kwa family of languages, especially the Grebo people of Liberia. When anyone dies, it is customary to put down The Mat physically. Mourners, especially women, sit on The Mat, wailing throughout the entire burial ceremony which may take up to two weeks. The grief of mourning is laid to rest on The Mat.

NGANLUN
The main stream from which we drink in my hometown of Tugbakeh.

WAHYEE
A popular young people's dance in the 1960s among a group of Grebo people, meant to be performed at parties.

YARKPAWOLLO
A defected Liberian soldier who terrorized the people of Liberia in 1965, and was fatally shot by government troops.

Photo by James Palmore

Patricia Jabbeh Wesley was born in Tugbakeh, Maryland County, Liberia (West Africa), and grew up in Monrovia. From 1983-1985, she studied at Indiana University in Bloomington, Indiana, where she earned a Master of Science degree in English Education before returning to her native country. Wesley and her family were caught in Liberia's seven year civil war that began in 1989, and for the next two years witnessed the destruction of everything they knew. In 1991, Wesley, her husband Mlen-Too, and their children escaped the fighting and moved to Michigan, where they now live.